CALIFORNIA

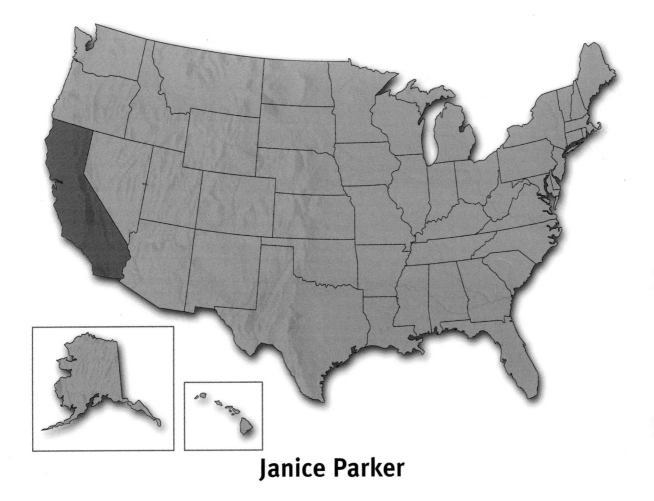

Janice Parker

Published by Weigl Publishers Inc.
123 South Broad Street, Box 227
Mankato, MN   56002
USA

Library of Congress Cataloguing-in-Publication Data available upon request from the publisher. Fax: (507)388-2746 for the attention of the Publishing Records Department.

ISBN 1-930954-45-X

Printed in the United States of America
1 2 3 4 5 6 7 8 9 0   05 04 03 02 01

Editor
Rennay Craats
Design
Warren Clark
Copy Editor
Heather Kissock
Cover Design
Terry Paulhus
Layout
Derek Heck

Photograph Credits
Every reasonable effort has been made to trace ownership and to obtain permission to reprint copyright material. The publishers would be pleased to have any errors or omissions brought to their attention so that they may be corrected in subsequent printings.

Cover: Water-skier (Eyewire), Grapes (Corel); **Archive Photos:** pages 3B-R, 17T, 19T-L (American Stock), 19B-L, 19R, 22B-L (Jeff Greenberg), 22T-L (Santi Visalli Inc.), 25T-L (Popperfoto), 25R (Lee), 27R (Reuters/Sam Mircovich), 27B (Reuters/Sam Mircovich), **California Division of Tourism:** pages 7R (Robert Holmes), 8T-L (Robert Holmes), 9T-R (Robert Holmes), 10T-L (Carrie Grant), 10B-L (Robert Holmes), 10R (Robert Holmes), 11B-R (Robert Holmes), 12B-L (Robert Holmes), 14B-L (Robert Holmes), 20B-L (Robert Holmes), 21B-L (Robert Holmes), 23B-L (Robert Holmes), 23R (Robert Holmes), 25B-L (Robert Holmes), 26T-L (Robert Holmes), 28B (Robert Holmes), 29B (Robert Holmes); **California Office of Tourism:** pages 4R (Robert Holmes), 6 B-L (Robert Holmes), 8B-L (Robert Holmes), 26B-L (Robert Holmes), 26B-R (Robert Holmes); **Corel Corporation:** 11B-L, 14T-L, 15T-L; **Courtesy Newport Conference & Visitors Bureau:** pages 3 T-L and 7B (John Connell), 7TL; **Eilleen L. Bowen:** pages 16R, 24B-L; **Globe Photos Inc:** page 24T-L, 24R; **Los Angeles Convention and Visitors Bureau:** pages 5T-L (Michele & Tom Grimm), 27L (Michele & Tom Grimm); **Morro Bay State Park Museum of Natural History:** page 16B-L (H.L. Barnes); **Photos Courtesy Eureka! Humbolt County Convention and Visitors Bureau:** pages 3M-L and 10T-L (Carrie Grant), 4T-L (Carrie Grant), 5B-L (Carrie Grant), 6T-L (Don Leonard), 9B-L (Jack Hopkins), 16T-L (Miya Benjamin); **PhotoDisk:** page 13T-L; **PlanetWare:** pages 3B-L, 3T-R, 6R, 9T-R, 9B-R, 11T-L, 12T-L, 12R, 13B-L, 14R, 15B, 18T, 18B, 20T-L, 20R, 21B, 22R, 23T-L, 28L, 28R; **Tom Myers Photography:** pages 4B-L (Tom Myers), 13R (Sally Myers), 15R (Tom Myers), 21T-L (Tom Myers), 29T (Tom Myers); **U.S. National Park Service, Cabrillo National Monument:** pages 17B-L, 17R.

CONTENTS

INTRODUCTION

California's warm climate, beautiful landscapes, and exciting attractions draw tourists from around the world. California is the third largest state in area in the United States, and it has the most people. No other state has such varied geography, climate, and population. Beautiful beaches, rocky cliffs, snowy mountains, barren deserts, and lush forests are all within close distance from one another.

QUICK FACTS

California's nickname, the Golden State, comes from the importance of the gold rush to its history.

California entered the Union on September 9, 1850. It was the thirty-first state.

California's state bird is the California Valley Quail.

The state flag was adopted in 1911. It has a red star and the state animal, a grizzly bear, standing on a green area. There is a red strip along the bottom with the words "California Republic" written above it.

Venice Beach is a popular tourist location in California.

The state motto is "Eureka," meaning "I have found it."

Los Angeles International Airport is the third busiest airport in the country.

Getting There

California is located on the Pacific Coast. It shares its borders with Oregon to the north, Nevada and Arizona to the east, and Mexico to the south.

There are many different ways to reach California. Airports, including those in Los Angeles, San Diego, San Jose, San Francisco, and Oakland, receive flights from around the world. Local airports have **domestic** flights throughout California as well as flights across the country.

Train travelers can arrive on various rail lines that end up in large cities including Los Angeles and San Francisco. Passenger trains stop in about forty California cities. The many freeways and highways in California make car travel easy.

QUICK FACTS

The state seal was adopted in 1848. It shows miners, who represent the state's mineral resources. Wheat and grapes represent Californian agriculture, and ships represent **merchants**.

The California Redwood is the state tree.

California is the third largest state after Alaska and Texas.

Location Map

Sacramento

San Francisco

CALIFORNIA

Los Angeles

San Diego

N

| 0 | 240 | 480 | 720 | 960 | 1200 Miles |
| 0 | 480 | 960 | 1440 | 1920 Kms |

Since the gold rush brought many people to the state, California's population has grown. The large population is made up of **diverse** cultural and ethnic groups. The hispanic culture in particular can be found throughout the state. You are just as likely to eat a **burrito** as a hamburger in most parts of the state. California also has diverse income groups. There are many multi-millionaires in the state. There are also large groups of low-income families and individuals.

Victorian architecture accents San Francisco's steep streets.

QUICK FACTS

The state flower is the golden poppy.

The geographic center of California is in Madera County, 35 miles northeast of Madera.

California has eighteen national forests and 264 state parks and beaches.

PAGE

1600

ASHBU

California is famous for its entertainment industry. Many motion pictures and television programs are created and filmed in the state. Movie stars can be seen walking down the street in many California cities. People from all over North America move to California in hopes of becoming actors, screenwriters, or directors.

Disneyland also attracts people from around the world. Other people move to the state simply because they love the warm climate and friendly people. California is known for its healthy lifestyles and fresh food.

Disneyland is often called the "happiest place on Earth."

Tidal pools are home to many crab and fish species.

LAND AND CLIMATE

California is divided into eight main regions, which include deserts, valleys, and mountain ranges formed from volcanoes. The San Andreas Fault is a fracture in the earth that runs through the state. When the earth's crust moves along this and other faults, an earthquake occurs. Throughout history, California has experienced some very destructive earthquakes.

With so many landscapes, California also has many different climates. There are five types of climate in the state: coastal, valley, foothill, mountain, and desert. Southern coastal areas are sunny and warm with mild winters. Northern coastal areas are also mild but cooler. The valley and foothill areas are hot and dry in the summer and cold and humid in the winter. Summers in the mountain areas are warm. The desert areas are very dry and hot.

The average July temperature in California is 75° F, and the average January temperature drops to 44° F. Winters are rainy or even snowy as the **elevation** increases. Tamarack in the Sierra Nevada sees 450 inches of snowfall each year. Other areas see virtually no rain at all. From October 3, 1912, to November 8, 1914, areas of Death Valley received no precipitation. This 760-day rainless stretch set a United States record.

QUICK FACTS

The foothill areas rarely have snow.

The San Andreas Fault is 600 miles long and is up to 1 mile wide in places.

California has the highest and lowest points in mainland United States: Mount Whitney is 14,494 feet above sea level, while Death Valley is 282 feet below sea level.

The lowest recorded temperature in California was -45° F. The highest recorded temperature in America occurred in California. It reached 134° F.

Topographical Map

N

0	150	300	450	600	750	Miles
0		300	600	900	1200	Kms

NATURAL RESOURCES

Timber is an important natural resource in California. More than two-fifths of the state is forest land with mostly fir, pine, redwood, and oak trees.

The state is rich in marine life, such as crabs and tuna. Fish, shellfish, lobsters, and shrimp are caught off the coast of California and sold in the rest of the country.

The earth in California is another important resource. Cement, sand, gravel, and stone are mined in **quarries** and used throughout the United States. The mild climate and rich soil help produce excellent crops. California has around 7.4 million acres of farmland. That is more than any other state.

Water in the ocean, rivers, and lakes are important resources for agriculture and tourism. California's many rivers help provide power through hydroelectricity.

Apricots are grown and dried in California. They are an excellent source of Vitamin A.

QUICK FACTS

California has many deposits of natural gas and petroleum.

California has more than 1,000 dams on its rivers to help control floods and store water for use in the long, dry summers or during droughts.

Approximately 10 percent of rain and dam water runoff in California is used in urban areas by residences, businesses, and the government.

PLANTS AND ANIMALS

California's plant and animal life is as varied as its geography and climate. Northern California has woodlands that contain some of the world's tallest trees—the coastal redwoods. Giant sequoia trees in the Sierra Nevada region are some of the largest trees in the world. Their trunks can be more than 39 feet across. Other common trees are oak, aspen, palm, and eucalyptus.

Common plants are the flowering dogwood and myrtle. The desert areas contain many different species of **succulents**. The state flower, the golden poppy, grows in the Central Valley. Creosote and mesquite are some of the few plants that can survive in the hot, dry climate of Death Valley.

California poppies are a native wildflower to the state. Other wildflowers include the giant wake robin and the checker lily.

The state is home to many different types of animals. Marine animals, such as sea lions, otters, seals, and whales can be found off the coast. The desert areas are home to coyotes, hares, lizards, and bighorn sheep. Cougars, black bears, and bobcats live in the forests. Many different bird species spend all or part of the year in California. Seagulls, terns, and pelicans live along the coast. Spotted owls live in the northern forest areas.

The **endangered** California condor is one of the largest birds in the world. Only a few survive in the wild. Once there were hundreds of these birds in the state. As their **habitat** was disturbed and destroyed, the condors began to die out. In 1982, there were only twenty-three of the birds left. Conservation groups are trying to save the California condor by breeding them in **captivity** and releasing them into the wild. Several other Californian animals are endangered, including the San Joaquin kit fox, the gray wolf, and the black-footed ferret.

QUICK FACTS

The grizzly bear is the state animal, but it has not been found in California since the last one was shot in 1922.

California condors weigh about 20 pounds and have a wingspan of 9 feet.

Every year in the middle of March, thousands of swallows return to the San Juan Capistrano area.

Bighorn sheep usually live on rocky or grassy mountain slopes. They are excellent climbers.

TOURISM

Tourism is a widespread and important industry in California. The state's eight national parks are some of the most popular in the country. The three largest cities, Los Angeles, San Francisco, and San Diego, attract many tourists from elsewhere in the country and around the world.

Disneyland is one of the world's most famous theme parks. Since it opened in 1955, millions of people have visited the park. Many tourists also visit Hollywood in Los Angeles. It is the center of the American motion picture industry.

The San Diego Zoo is one of the largest zoos in the world. The zoo is known for displaying its animals in natural surroundings.

The coast of California attracts visitors from around the world. They come for the beautiful beaches and sports, such as surfing, windsurfing, and sailing.

QUICK FACTS

More than 2,000 names of entertainment stars line the Hollywood Walk of Fame.

Universal Studios is the largest film studio in the world. Visitors can take a tram tour that takes them into the heart of fires and earthquakes, or face-to-face with the mechanical shark from the film, *Jaws*.

The Golden Gate Bridge is a **landmark** in San Francisco.

The San Diego Zoo is known for its preservation of endangered species. The zoo has more than 4,000 animals.

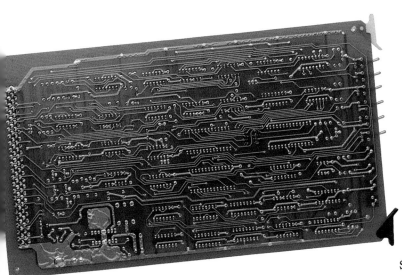

INDUSTRY

Manufacturing, tourism, and agriculture are some of the leading industries in California. The motion picture industry provides jobs for many Californians. Actors, directors, screenwriters, camera operators, and special effects staff all help to create films.

A 20-mile strip near San Jose, called Silicon Valley, is known for its high-technology industry. The area is named after the material silicon, which is used to make microchips. Many companies design and manufacture microchips, which are used in computers and other electronics equipment. The first compact, personal computers to be used in homes and offices were released in 1976 by Apple Computers, a company created by Los Altos native Steve Jobs.

The high-technology industry is developing at a rapid rate. Americans rely heavily on high-technology products in their everyday lives.

QUICK FACTS

Levi's jeans were first made in California in 1874 by Levi Strauss.

Many television programs are made in and around Los Angeles.

One in every five Californians works in the high-technology industry.

The film industry brings in $28 million per year and employs 475,000 Californians.

Los Angeles is known for its bad air pollution. A gray cloud of smog from the many cars and industrial plants sits over the city.

GOODS AND SERVICES

Some of the best wine in the world is produced in northern California in the Napa, Sonoma, and Mendocino counties. The soil and climate are perfect for vineyards. Grapes are the second leading farm product, next to milk and cream products.

America's almonds, pistachios, walnuts, kiwi fruit, dates, and olives come almost entirely from California. The state also produces more greenhouse and nursery products, such as potted plants and cut flowers, than any other.

California is the top American state for manufacturing. Factories make processed foods, electronics equipment, and transportation equipment, including cars and aircraft.

The Napa Valley is home to some of the most famous vineyards and wineries in the world. California supplies 90 percent of the grape crops in the United States.

QUICK FACTS

If California were a country, its GDP, **gross domestic product**, would be one of the highest of any country in the world.

California grows 55 percent of the fruits, nuts, and vegetables in the United States.

California has more motor vehicles for its area and more multilane divided highways than anywhere else in the world.

QUICK FACTS

California is the only place in the U.S. that produces tungsten, a mineral used in electronics.

In 1999, 396 million gallons of Californian wine were sold in the United States.

California produced many of the ships and aircraft used during World War II.

Gold mining played an important role in the history of the state. Just about one week before Mexico handed California over to the United States, gold was discovered in the state. In 1849, people in search of gold—called Forty-Niners—came to California from all over the world. By the end of that year, 90,000 people lived in the state. Three years later, the population had grown to 220,000. The gold rush ended almost as quickly as it began. By 1854, it was mostly over. California continues to produce more gold than most other states.

The service industries make up more than three-quarters of the total value of all goods and services in California. Service industry jobs are varied, including actors, screenwriters, doctors, schoolteachers, and bus drivers.

Prospectors found gold nuggets in streams and rivers. When rock erodes, the gold falls to the bottom of the riverbed.

Amtrak and the electronic trolley coaches provide rail transportation in the San Diego area.

FIRST NATIONS

Some scientists believe that about 15,000 years ago, people crossed from what is now Siberia to North America over a land bridge that is now covered in water. These people spread across North and South America. The Native peoples in California were isolated from others on the continent by the high mountains. By the sixteenth century, the area that is now California had the greatest concentration of Native people in North America.

The early Native groups included the Hupa, who lived in the far northwest. The Ohlone people lived in the San Francisco area, and the Pomo to the north. The Maidu peoples occupied central California, and the Quechan lived in the south. Some of the other Native groups were the Cahiulla, Chumash, Karok, Mojave, Yokut, Paiute, and Modoc. In all, the Native peoples spoke twenty-one different languages and more than one hundred **dialects**. The different groups usually lived at peace with one another.

QUICK FACTS

Early peoples fished, hunted for game, and gathered nuts, seeds, and berries.

Native people in northern California made baskets for carrying food and infants. Those who lived near the coast used shells as money.

Before the Europeans arrived in California, there were as many as 300,000 Native Americans. By 1900, there were only 16,000. About 60 percent died from new diseases brought by the Europeans.

Pictographs or cave paintings tell stories of people who lived many years ago.

EXPLORERS

In 1542, Juan Rodriguez Cabrillo, a Portuguese sailor, sailed into San Diego Bay and became the first European to reach the land he named California. About 40 years later, British explorer Sir Francis Drake traveled to the San Francisco area. Drake claimed the land for England by leaving an engraved brass plate. The brass plate was not found until 1937, so England's claim was not recognized. His visit encouraged the Spanish to return to the area.

Francisco Gali discovered Monterey Bay in 1584. Eight years later, Sebastian Vizcaino explored the coast of California. He reported his findings back to Spain, urging the king to create a colony in the area. However, it was not until 1769 that a Spanish **expedition** was sent to California again.

In 1825, an American explorer, Captain John C. Fremont, led two surveying groups in the area. He raised an American flag near the Mexican government headquarters. More and more Americans moved into California. Mexico gave California to the United States after the Mexican–American war in 1848.

QUICK FACTS

The first European explorers to visit the San Francisco area missed the San Francisco Bay.

Spanish Franciscan friar Junipero Serra was a priest and explorer. He helped colonize California.

The Cabrillo National Monument is located in San Diego. It was built in 1913 to honor Cabrillo's accomplishments.

MISSIONARIES

The first mission, San Diego de Alcalá, was built near San Diego. By 1823, there were twenty-one missions from San Diego to Sonoma. The Spanish built military forts, called presidios, near many of the missions. Each mission was about one day's walk from the next. The **missionaries** tried to get the Native peoples to give up their own spiritual beliefs and adopt **Christianity**. Many Native peoples fought against the missionaries' beliefs and way of life. The missionaries taught many Native Americans how to grow wheat and other crops and how to care for cattle. Churches and farms were built with the help of the Native people.

QUICK FACTS

The Spanish government in Mexico sent friar Junipero Serra to California to build missions.

When California became part of Mexico in 1821, the Mexican government closed the missions and sold the land to Californios, who were wealthy Mexican **aristocrats**.

Fort Ross was built by Russian settlers who traveled to California. Today, Fort Ross is located in a national park.

EARLY SETTLERS

In 1812, Russian fur traders from Alaska moved south to the northwest coast of California. They set up Fort Ross about 60 miles north of San Francisco. They stayed there until 1841.

Just one week before Mexico handed California over to the United States, a man named James Marshall discovered gold. The gold rush of 1849 began. Thousands of people from across the country and Europe went to California hoping to strike gold. Most **prospectors** moved to areas near Sacramento or Stockton. San Francisco boomed. By the end of the gold rush, nearly $2 billion in gold had been found. Most prospectors found nothing. Many became merchants or farmers in the area.

Even after the gold rush ended, people continued to move to California. The transcontinental railroad, completed in 1869, made it easier and safer for people to travel across the country. During the Great Depression of the 1930s, people from all over the United States traveled to California with hopes of finding work and a better life.

QUICK FACTS

In 1906, an earthquake and fire destroyed most of San Francisco.

Most of California's new residents were men. Few women made the difficult trek across the country to pan for gold.

Miners who came to California for the gold rush sent their laundry to Honolulu, Hawaii. Costs in California were so high, it was cheaper to send shirts to Hawaii than to get them washed and pressed at home.

The Mother Lode is the name of the strip of land along the Sierra Nevada that was rich with gold-filled quartz.

Gold fever spread quickly to other parts of the world. The discovery of gold allowed cities such as San Francisco and Sacramento to develop and thrive.

POPULATION

Nearly one out of every eight people in the United States lives in California. California's population has grown very quickly since the beginning of the twentieth century. In 1900, the population was about 1.5 million. By 1950, it was 10.5 million. In 1990, the population of California tripled to 30 million.

Nearly 95 percent of Californians live in or near a major city. Most people live in southern California. The five counties in the southern part of the state have more people than the other fifty-three counties combined.

California is one of the most ethnically diverse states. Nearly one-quarter of the population is Latino, which include people with Mexican, Central American, South American, Cuban, and Puerto Rican backgrounds. About one in ten is from Asia, while African Americans make up about 7 percent of the population.

QUICK FACTS

More than 33 million people now live in California.

Richard Nixon, the thirty-seventh American president, was born in Yorba Linda, California.

Ronald Reagan was governor of California for two terms before he was the president of the United States.

California is the wealthiest state in the United States. It also has one of the worst poverty rates in the country.

California has thirty-five cities that have more than 100,000 people.

Buddhist temples are beautiful buildings. The architecture and design of these buildings are very detailed and colorful.

POLITICS AND GOVERNMENT

The California government is split into three branches. The executive branch makes sure that the state laws are carried out. The governor is the head of the executive branch. The legislative branch makes laws for the state. The legislature includes elected members that make up the Senate and the assembly. The judicial branch rules on legal cases in the state. The California Supreme Court is the state's highest court. There are many lower local courts.

California is divided into fifty-eight counties. Each county has its own elected board of supervisors. They usually have a sheriff, district attorney, and county clerk. Most of the more than 450 cities have a mayor and city council.

Each state has a state government building.

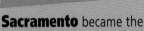

California has two seats in the U.S. Senate, and fifty-two seats in the U.S. House of Representatives.

CULTURAL GROUPS

Many different cultures live and work in the state. Latinos make up a large portion of the population in California. Most Latinos speak both English and Spanish. Latino culture exists throughout California. Mexican and South American food is enjoyed throughout the state. The large number of cities with Spanish names also reflect the Latino influence. California Latinos celebrate Cinco de Mayo on May 5. This Mexican holiday is known for its festive dancing, music, and food.

More new immigrants settle in California than in any other state. Most of the recent immigrants come from Asian countries, such as China or Japan, or the Pacific Islands, such as the Philippines. San Francisco has a large Chinese American community.

QUICK FACTS

More immigrants settle in California than any other state—it welcomed more than one-third of the nation's total immigrants in 1994.

California has the largest number of Spanish speakers, Chinese, Filipinos, Japanese, Koreans, Vietnamese, and Native Americans in the country. It has the second largest population of African Americans.

Tortillas are traditionally made and rolled out by hand. They are made with flour.

Each year in late January or early February, Chinese New Year is celebrated with the Golden Dragon parade and fireworks. San Francisco celebrates the New Year more than many other Californian cities because it has one of the largest Chinese populations in the country. Ancestor's Day, in early April, is a day when many Chinese Americans clean and decorate the graves of their ancestors. In September, the moon festival is a celebration of harvest time.

Japanese Americans are known for their beautiful art. **Calligraphy**, flower arranging, and sculptured landscapes are parts of the Japanese culture that have been brought to California.

African-American culture is also strong in California. Many African Americans moved to the state during World War II to find work. The music and fashions that come from African-American communities can be heard and seen across the state and country.

QUICK FACTS

More people live in California's urban areas than any other state. More than three-quarters of the population live in three metropolitan areas: Los Angeles–Long Beach–Anaheim, San Francisco–Oakland–San Jose, and San Diego.

The headquarters of the Buddhist Churches of America is in San Francisco.

Chinese New Year is celebrated throughout California.

ARTS AND ENTERTAINMENT

The motion picture industry, based in Hollywood, began in California at the end of the nineteenth century. Silent movies were made in the 1920s with actors such as Charlie Chaplin.

Walt Disney began his career by making a ten-minute cartoon about a mouse called Mickey. Disney followed with longer animated films, and his company is still very successful today.

California is a major center for the performing arts. It has many symphony orchestras, opera companies, and musicians. In the 1960s, groups such as the Beach Boys wrote songs about surfing and beaches. Millions of people listened to their "California sound." Today, all kinds of music are widespread in the state. Each year, many large music festivals take place in California, including the Monterey Jazz Festival, the Mozart Festival, and the Sacramento Jazz Festival.

QUICK FACTS

Californian photographer
Ansel Adams is known for his black and white nature pictures.

Some of the earliest
Californian artwork is the rock paintings made by the Native peoples who lived in the area more than 1,000 years ago.

Charlie Chaplin made his tramp character famous in silent movies. He was often called the funniest man in the world.

The first film studio in Hollywood opened in 1911 on the corner of Sunset and Gower. Soon after, people such as Cecil B. DeMille began to make films in the area, drawn by the warm climate and open spaces. During the 1920s and 1930s, the motion picture industry blossomed in Hollywood. Powerful film studios and famous movie stars made the area famous.

John Steinbeck won the Pulitzer Prize in 1940 for his novel *Grapes of Wrath*.

QUICK FACTS

In 1962, John Steinbeck received the Nobel Prize for Literature.

California is sometimes referred to as the entertainment capital of the world.

The Hollywood Walk of Fame began in 1960 with 2,500 blank stars. More than 2,100 of the stars have been filled with names of entertainment stars.

California has produced many writers, entertainers, and artists. Mark Twain, author of *The Adventures of Tom Sawyer* and *The Adventures of Huckleberry Finn*, lived in San Francisco. Jack London, who wrote *The Call of the Wild*, lived in the Sonoma Valley. John Steinbeck, author of *The Grapes of Wrath*, was born in Salinas. In the 1950s, the **Beat** generation began in San Francisco with poets and authors such as Jack Kerouac. Some modern Californian writers include Chinese-American author Amy Tan and the African-American author Alice Walker.

Amy Tan attended the University of California, Santa Cruz and Berkeley University.

SPORTS

California is the perfect place for many water sports. The warm climate and beautiful beaches help make swimming, sailing, and beach volleyball popular. Deep-sea diving allows people to view life in the ocean. California has the best locations in the country for surfing and windsurfing.

People can play tennis and golf year round in California. California has nearly 700 golf courses, including the famous Pebble Beach course. A person can golf one day, then go skiing in the nearby mountains the next.

QUICK FACTS

Each New Year's Day, Pasadena holds the Tournament of Roses. The event consists of a parade and the Rose Bowl, a college football game.

Yosemite National Park has perfect locations for rock climbing.

The first wetsuit for deep sea diving was created at the University of California in 1956.

In 2000, the Los Angeles Lakers won the NBA championships.

Palm Springs Golf Course is a public course with a resort and country club. It has been open since 1968.

Professional team sports are very popular in California. The state has three football, five baseball, four basketball, and three hockey teams. The San Francisco 49ers football team was the first major league professional sports team in California. In 1994, the 49ers set a National Football League record when they won their fifth Super Bowl championship. The Los Angeles Lakers have won the National Basketball Association title twelve times.

QUICK FACTS

The Los Angeles Lakers have retired the uniforms of several players, including Wilt Chamberlain (number 13), Kareem Abdul-Jabbar (number 33), and Magic Johnson (number 32).

Huntington Beach has the International Surfing Museum, which contains artifacts showing the history of the sport.

Beach volleyball was first played in Santa Monica in the 1920s.

Kayaking is a popular sport along the coast of California.

California has hosted several international sporting events. The Summer Olympics were in Los Angeles in 1932 and again in 1984. Squaw Valley hosted the Winter Olympics in 1960. The 1994 World Cup soccer games were held in Pasadena.

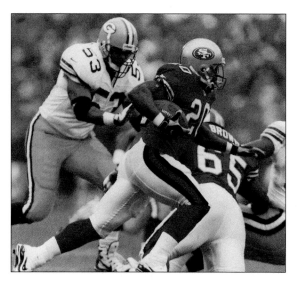

The San Francisco 49ers played their first game in 1950. This team has been very successful over the years.

Brain Teasers

2 What makes the Golden Gate Bridge, which spans the entrance of the San Francisco Bay, special?

Answer: Spanning 6,450 feet, it is one of the longest suspension bridges in the world.

1 Tall Trees

Which trees are the widest and tallest in the world?

Answer: Giant sequoias are the widest trees. Coastal redwoods are the tallest.

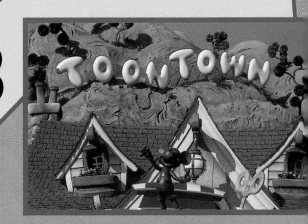

3

What year did Disneyland, also called the "Happiest Place on Earth," open?

Answer: It opened in 1955.

4 Directions

Put the following cities in order from north to south:

Los Angeles
Sacramento
Santa Barbara

San Francisco
San Diego
San Jose

Answer:
1. Sacramento
2. San Francisco
3. San Jose
4. Santa Barbara
5. Los Angeles
6. San Diego

5

What is the name of the fault that is the cause of earthquakes in California?

Answer: San Andreas fault

6

What is the zip code for many famous addresses in Beverly Hills?

Answer: 90210. The popular television show made those five numbers well known.

7

Which city has not been California's capital at some time during the state's history?

a) Sacramento   b) San Jose

c) San Diego   d) Monteray

Answer: c) San Diego

8

What is the Mother Lode in California?

Answer: The Mother Lode is the area along the Sierra Nevada that was rich in gold.

FOR MORE INFORMATION

Books

Altman, Linda Jacobs. *California: Celebrate the States*. New York: Benchmark Books, 1997.

Aylesworth, Thomas G. *The Pacific: California, Hawaii: Discovering America*. New York: Chelsea House, 1996.

Bock, Judy and Rachel Kranz. *Scholastic encyclopedia of the United States*. New York: Scholastic, 1997.

Heinrichs, Ann. *California: America the beautiful*. New York: Children's Press, 1998.

Hicks, Roger. *The Big Book of America*. Philadelphia: Courage Books, 1994.

Web Sites

There are many great web sites on the Internet about California. Here are a few you can look at to find out more about this amazing state.

The Official California Home Page
http://www.ca.gov

California State Parks
http://cal-parks.ca.gov

50 States: California
www.50states.com/california.htm

Tour California
www.gocalif.ca.gov/index2.html

Some web sites stay current longer than others. To find more California web sites, use your Internet search engines to look up such topics as "California," "Los Angeles Lakers," "San Andreas fault," or any other topic you want to research.

GLOSSARY

aristocrats: people from nobility or the ruling class

Beat: generation in the 1950s that focused on mysticism and relaxed social inhibitions

burrito: a flour tortilla folded over a filling, often of meat, cheese, or refried beans

calligraphy: the art of writing beautifully with ink and a brush

captivity: not in the wild

Christianity: the belief in the life and worship of Jesus Christ as the son of God

conservation: protecting the environment

dialects: regional versions of a language

diverse: made up of many different qualities or elements

domestic: pertaining to one's own country and not others

elevation: height above sea level

endangered: in danger of becoming extinct

expedition: a long trip, usually to explore

gross domestic product: the amount of money a country makes from its exports

habitat: the place where a plant or animal lives and grows

landmark: a place of historical or cultural importance

merchants: people who buy and sell goods

missionaries: people sent to another country to do charitable work and convert others to their religion

prospectors: people searching a region for gold

quarries: large areas where stone is obtained

succulents: fleshy plants that are found in desert areas and can store water in their leaves

suspension: when something is held in place from above rather than supported from below

INDEX